SOCCER BIOGRAPHIES

AITANA BONMATÍ

KENNY ABDO

Fly!
An Imprint of Abdo Zoom
abdobooks.com

abdobooks.com

Published by Abdo Zoom, a division of ABDO, P.O. Box 398166, Minneapolis, Minnesota 55439.

Printed in the United States of America, North Mankato, Minnesota.
052025
092025

THIS BOOK CONTAINS RECYCLED MATERIALS

Photo Credits: Alamy, AP Images, Getty Images, Shutterstock
Production Contributors: Kenny Abdo, Jennie Forsberg, Grace Hansen
Design Contributors: Candice Keimig, Neil Klinepier, Victoria Bates

Library of Congress Control Number: 2024947815

Publisher's Cataloging-in-Publication Data

Names: Abdo, Kenny, author.
Title: Aitana Bonmati / by Kenny Abdo
Description: Minneapolis, Minnesota : Abdo Zoom, 2026 | Series: Soccer biographies | Includes online resources and index.
Identifiers: ISBN 9781098288839 (lib. bdg.) | ISBN 9781098289539 (ebook) | ISBN 9781098289881 (Read-to-me ebook)
Subjects: LCSH: Women soccer players--Biography--Juvenile literature. | Soccer players--Biography--Juvenile literature. | Professional athletes--Biography-Juvenile literature. | Futbol Club Barcelona--Juvenile literature.
Classification: DDC 796.334092--dc23

TABLE OF CONTENTS

AITANA BONMATÍ

As Barcelona's clutch midfielder, Aitana Bonmatí's skills set a gold standard for soccer in every match!

EARLY YEARS

Bonmatí was born in 1998 in Sant Pere de Ribes, Spain. She loved playing sports from a young age. Her parents supported her passion for soccer. Bonmatí was determined to be the best player in the world.

Bonmatí's impressive skills caught the attention of FC Barcelona's youth academy. By 2016, she was invited to play for the club's official team!

GOING PRO

Bonmatí hit the field with her impressive skills as a midfielder. She helped her team win the 2017 **Copa de la Reina**! That season, Barcelona finished as runners-up in the **UEFA** Women's **Champions League**.

STANLEY

In 2018, Bonmatí helped **clinch** another **Copa de la Reina**. She continued to shine when Barcelona won the 2019 **Primera División** title. Bonmatí also helped the team reach another **Champions League** final to secure a **Spanish Super Cup**!

Barcelona reached the finals of the 2020 **UEFA** Women's **Champions League**. In 2021, they secured a **treble**: the **Primera División**, **Copa de la Reina**, and UEFA Women's Champions League.

INNERS
N'S CHAMPIONS LEAGUE 2020/21
FCB
GOTHENBURG

Emirates
FLY BETTER
STANLEY

In 2022, Bonmatí injured her right leg. This kept her out of a several games. When she returned on the field, Bonmatí scored the game-winning goal against SD Eibar. By the end of the season, the team secured another **Copa de la Reina**!

Before the 2022–23 season, Alexia Putellas was injured. Barcelona's main midfielder had to sit out. Bonmatí took her place and had an incredible season.

ENGLAND
20 AUGUST 2023
SYDNEY

Barcelona won every tournament Bonmatí played in and was named player of the match each time. She capped off the season with a Ballon d'Or Féminin!

During the 2023–24 season, the team kept performing well. With Bonmatí's leadership, Barcelona reached the 2024 Champion of the Nations League. They beat France 2–0, with Bonmatí scoring one goal. She was named MVP of the match.

That same season, Barcelona secured their second **treble**. The team also won their first **continental quadruple**! Bonmatí had six assists and six goals, earning the title of player of the tournament!

Spotify

LEGACY

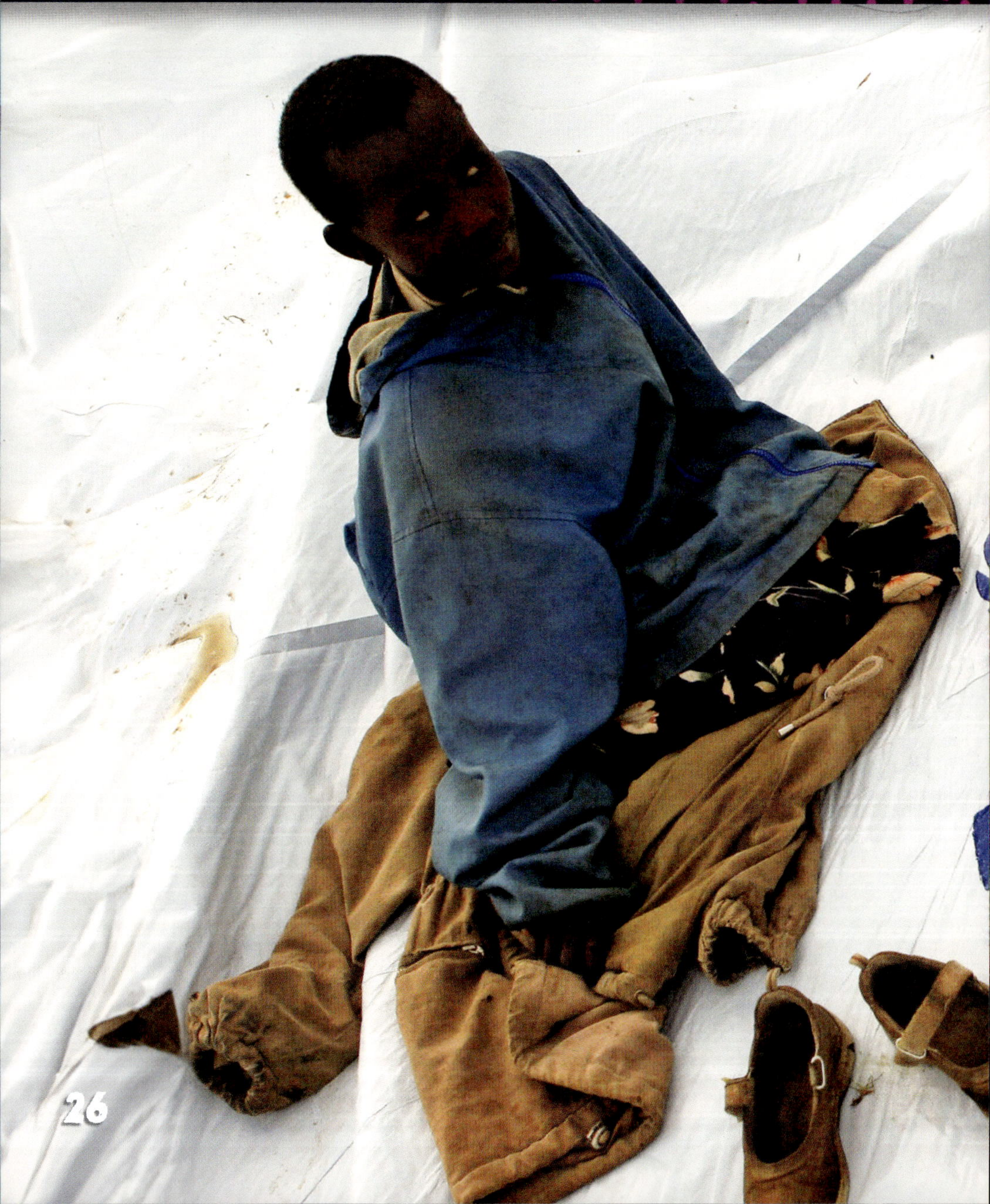

Since 2022, Bonmatí has supported the UNHCR. This organization helps **refugees** return home. She is also an **ambassador** for the Barça Foundation.

Bonmatí continues to weave her magic on the field, dribbling past defenders and inspiring younger generations of girls with her greatness. She is truly in a league of her own!

GLOSSARY

ambassador – anyone who is sent as a representative or messenger.

Champions League – a yearly soccer competition organized by the UEFA.

clinch – to confirm a win.

continental quadruple – when a soccer team wins four titles or cups in a single season.

Copa de la Reina – a yearly soccer tournament for women's teams in Spain.

Primera División – the top league for women's soccer.

refugee – a person forced to leave his or her home or country to seek safety or protection.

Spanish Super Cup – a yearly soccer match organized by UEFA between the winners of the Champions League and the Europa League.

treble – when a soccer team wins three titles or cups in a single season.

UEFA – short for Union of European Football Associations.

ONLINE RESOURCES

Booklinks
NONFICTION NETWORK
FREE! ONLINE NONFICTION RESOURCES

To learn more about Aitana Bonmatí, please visit abdobooklinks.com or scan this QR code. These links are routinely monitored and updated to provide the most current information available.

INDEX